The Positive Aspects of Long Term Hospitalization in the Public Sector for Chronic Psychiatric Patients

Formulated by the Committee on Psychopathology
Group for the Advancement of Psychiatry

Mental Health Materials Center
30 E. 29th Street, New York, NY 10016

Library of Congress Cataloging in Publication Data

Main entry under title:

Group for the Advancement of Psychiatry. Committee on Psychopathology.

The positive aspects of long term hospitalization in the public sector for chronic psychiatric patients.

(Publication / Group for the Advancement of Psychiatry; v. 11 no. 110)

Includes bibliographical references.

1. Mentally ill——Institutional care. 2.Chronically ill— Institutional care. 3. Psychiatric hospital care. 4. Long-term care of the sick. I. Title. II. Series: Publication (Group for the Advancement of Psychiatry); v. 11, no. 110.

RC480.53.G76   1982   362.2'1   82-14389

ISBN 0-910958-15-7

September, 1982, Volume XI, Publication No. 110

This is the fourth in a series of publications comprising Volume XI.

For information on availability of this publication, please contact the Mental Health Materials Center, 30 East 29th Street, New York, NY 10016.

Manufactured in the United States of America

CONTENTS

WITHDRAWN

STATEMENT OF PURPOSE

THE GROUP FOR THE ADVANCEMENT OF PSYCHIATRY has a membership of approximately 300 psychiatrists, most of whom are organized in the form of a number of working committees. These committees direct their efforts toward the study of various aspects of psychiatry and the application of this knowledge to the fields of mental health and human relations.

Collaboration with specialists in other disciplines has been and is one of GAP's working principles. Since the formation of GAP in 1946 its members have worked closely with such other specialists as anthropologists, biologists, economists, statisticians, educators, lawyers, nurses, psychologists, sociologists, social workers, and experts in mass communication, philosophy, and semantics. GAP envisages a continuing program of work according to the following aims:

1. To collect and appraise significant data in the fields of psychiatry, mental health, and human relations

2. To reevaluate old concepts and to develop and test new ones

3. To apply the knowledge thus obtained for the promotion of mental health and good human relations.

GAP is an independent group, and its reports represent the composite findings and opinions of its members only, guided by its many consultants.

THE POSITIVE ASPECTS OF LONG TERM HOSPITALIZATION IN THE PUBLIC SECTOR FOR CHRONIC PSYCHIATRIC PATIENTS was formulated by the Committee on Psychopathology, which acknowledges on page xi the participation of others in the preparation of this report. The members of this committee are listed below. The following pages list the members of the other GAP committees as well as additional membership categories and current and past officers of GAP.

COMMITTEE ON PSYCHOPATHOLOGY

David A. Adler, Boston, Mass., Chairperson
Wagner H. Bridger, Bronx, N.Y.
Doyle I. Carson, Dallas, Tex.
Paul E. Huston, Iowa City, Iowa
Richard E. Renneker, Los Angeles, Calif.

COMMITTEE ON ADOLESCENCE

Warren J. Gadpaille, Englewood, Colo.,
  Chairperson
Ian A. Canino, New York, N.Y.
Harrison P. Eddy, New York, N.Y.
Sherman C. Feinstein, Highland Park, Ill.
*Maurice R. Friend, New York, N.Y.
Michael Kalogerakis, New York, N.Y.
Clarice J. Kestenbaum, New York, N.Y.
Derek Miller, Chicago, Ill.
Silvio J. Onesti, Jr., Belmont, Mass.

COMMITTEE ON AGING

Charles M. Gaitz, Houston, Tex., Chairperson
Gene D. Cohen, Rockville, Md.
Lawrence F. Greenleigh, Los Angeles, Calif.
George H. Pollock, Chicago, Ill.
Harvey L. Ruben, New Haven, Conn.
F. Conyers Thompson, Jr., Atlanta, Ga.
*Jack Weinberg, Chicago, Ill.

COMMITTEE ON CHILD PSYCHIATRY

John F. McDermott, Jr., Honolulu, Hawaii,
  Chairperson
Paul L. Adams, Louisville, Ky.
James M. Bell, Canaan, N.Y.

*Deceased

Harlow Donald Dunton, New York, N.Y.
Joseph Fischoff, Detroit, Mich.
Joseph M. Green, Madison, Wis.
John Schowalter, New Haven, Conn.
Theodore Shapiro, New York, N.Y.
Peter Tanguay, Los Angeles, Calif.
Lenore F. C. Terr, San Francisco, Calif.

COMMITTEE ON THE COLLEGE STUDENT

Kent E. Robinson, Towson, Md.,
  Chairperson
Robert L. Arnstein, Hamden, Conn.
Varda Backus, La Jolla, Calif.
Myron B. Liptzin, Chapel Hill, N.C.
Malkah Tolpin Notman, Brookline, Mass.
Gloria C. Onque, Pittsburgh, Pa.
Elizabeth Aub Reid, Cambridge, Mass.
Earle Silber, Chevy Chase, Md.

COMMITTEE ON CULTURAL PSYCHIATRY

Andrea K. Delgado, New York, N.Y.,
  Chairperson
John P. Spiegel, Waltham, Mass.
Ronald M. Wintrob, Farmington, Conn.

COMMITTEE ON THE FAMILY

Henry U. Grunebaum, Cambridge, Mass.,
  Chairperson
W. Robert Beavers, Dallas, Tex.
Ellen M. Berman, Merion, Pa.
Lee Combrinck-Graham, Philadelphia, Pa.
Ira D. Glick, New York, N.Y.
Frederick Gottlieb, Los Angeles, Calif.
Charles A. Malone, Cleveland, Ohio
Joseph Satten, San Francisco, Calif.

COMMITTEE ACKNOWLEDGMENTS

In the preparation of this report, the Committee wishes to acknowledge the assistance of David Soskis who since its completion has gone on inactive status as a contributing member. We also wish to express our appreciation for the contributions in the formulation of this document of our two Ginsburg Fellows, Jeffrey Berland and James Ellison.

David A. Adler, Chairman

1

INTRODUCTION

The mental health system in the United States is an exceedingly complex and multifaceted system with multiple components both psychiatric and nonpsychiatric, public and private, providing treatment for very diverse problems of mental health and illness. One segment of the population of longstanding concern is those seriously disturbed individuals in need of community attention. Such individuals, many who evidence psychotic symptomatology and who are often labeled as "chronic mental patients," receive care within a wide arena of the mental health system. In this report we shall focus on the role of the hospital in the treatment of psychotic patients with chronic psychiatric disabilities. We shall argue that at least a segment of chronic mental patients require treatment functions best given in hospitals which provide longterm care. We must recognize that one cannot prevent chronicity, nor cure dependent chronic mental patients, many of whom will need indefinite care.[1-13]

The history of the chronic mental patient in America begins with the history of the United States itself and continues during various cycles of community versus hospital treatment. During the 1700's and early 1800's seriously ill people were the responsibility of towns and counties and were treated in prisons, almhouses, kept at home, or left to wander the countryside. Drawing upon the European humanitarian efforts and scientific observations of Tuke, Pinel, and others in the 1830's, Benjamin Rush led the first mental health reform movement in America, "the era of moral treatment." In the 1830's and 1840's a number of small hospitals providing caring environments and utilizing milieu techniques were established. In the 1840's, Horace Mann

1

and Dorothea Dix argued that the states should increase the number of therapeutic institutions for chronic mental patients. Dix powerfully demonstrated to state legislators that the community was neglecting these patients.

Moral treatment however was never universally adopted. By the late 1800's the state hospitals became anonymous institutions in which patients were committed, neglected, and abused. From the beginning, the new hospitals' budgets were inadequate. The hospitals quickly became unable to keep up with the dramatic increase in the United States population resulting in part from waves of new immigrants. Ideological issues including social Darwinism, a belief in biological determinism, and the work ethic; economic recession; as well as the rise of the industrial revolution furthered the notion that a large cost efficient custodial system was economically sound, and morally and scientifically correct.[12] The notion was irresistible. Even while the post-World War II era witnessed a massive influx of financing for psychiatric training and service programs, the warehousing of chronic psychotic patients increased in numbers until its peak in 1955 with some 560,000 patients in state and county mental hospitals across the country. While there has been a sharp decline to under 141,000 in 1979 in total resident patients, the rate of episodes of inpatient care has remained stable.[13–15]

In the 1950's, attempts were made to formulate a federal mental health policy that to date remains incomplete. In 1955, the Congress established the Joint Commission for Mental Health. Its report in 1961 recommended direct federal support for the treatment of the mentally ill.[16] In the 1960's the Community Mental Health Center's Act and its amendments became part of the Kennedy/Johnson attempt to enhance the entry of disadvantaged groups into America's political life. The decrease in state hospital census that began in 1955 resulted from advances in psychopharmacology, social psychiatry, psychotherapy, milieu treatment, the dawning of an era emphasizing civil liberties, and a shift in the locus of care, as much as any impact of the community mental health movement. The escalation of hospital per diem costs was one of several important economic factors in the movement to eliminate longterm public hospitalization. Community Mental Health Centers did provide necessary services to previously unserved and under-served populations particularly outpatients; however the seriously ill chronic psychiatric patient remained inadequately served.[17, 18] CMHC's neither had the resources nor the priority directive to do so. The 1970's witnessed a decline of faith in the community mental health movement. A new Commission on Mental Health documented the problems encountered by the community mental health center program.[19] As a result of its 1978 report to the President, the Community Mental Health Centers Act of 1980 was passed, but was effectively repealed in 1981. All this time the cost of psychiatric care was increasing. Not only has the argument of cost savings in community treatment remained unconvincing, but the nation is now in the throes of reorienting its priorities away from the governmental funding of human services.[4-6, 8, 11, 16-38]

The above brief historical review has focused attention on some of the loci of psychiatric care during the past 200 years. As we turn to patients (both adults and children) and their needs, it is apparent that many patients with a variety of psychiatric problems both require and benefit from psychiatric hospitalization of varying duration. These problems may be grouped descriptively:

- The patient with a *sudden loss of contact with reality*, including the acutely psychotic schizophrenic and manic patient; the chronic psychotic patient in acute decompensation; the organic patient with psychosis as a consequence of illness, substance abuse, etc.
- The *patient in need of detoxification* as a consequence of substance abuse.
- The *undiagnosed patient* in need of diagnostic clarification.
- The *self-destructive patient* including a wide spectrum of

patients with chronic psychoses, severe characterologic problems, major depressions, suicidality, and acting out in adolescence.

- The *assaultive/dangerous patient*, including the acute and chronic psychotic, the antisocial character, and the severely disturbed adolescent.
- The *court-committed involuntary patient* for whom diagnostic observation, competency determination, or treatment is mandated.
- The *non-dangerous vulnerable chronic mental patient* including the patient with a definitive diagnosis of psychosis, the severely retarded, and the chronically institutionalized.
- The *confused or demented geriatric patient* who loses the ability to function independently and needs a comprehensive assessment.
- A group of patients with acute severe psychiatric difficulties for whom there is *no adequate support system*.
- A group of patients who are *unable to cope with severe life stresses*, including patients from a broad diagnostic spectrum (severe neuroses, panic attacks, severe character problems, anorexia nervosa, etc.)

For many of the above groups there is little argument about the value of acute short-term psychiatric hospitalization (as defined by a period of hospitalization of 30 or even 60 days[40]) in helping people recover from acute psychiatric problems that interfere with or endanger their lives or the lives of those around them. But what of the patient whose care necessitates *longterm* or even indefinite care which may be best provided in a hospital?

For the purposes of this report, longterm hospitalization is used to indicate a need for hospitalization that has a minimum time limit of six months, but may extend onwards to no expectable end. For some chronic patients, a prolonged period of hospitalization may be necessary to implement treatment plans, modify the external environment, or try out new treatment interventions. For others longterm hospitalization without foreseeable discharge may be necessary to provide adequate protective custodial care.

In 1969, GAP published a report entitled *Crisis in Psychiatric Hospitalization*[39] which emphasized the essential place of the psychiatric hospital as part of the continuum in comprehensive general psychiatric services. In that report the positive aspects of psychiatric hospitalization were reviewed. Indications for hospitalization; diagnostic, protective, and therapeutic interventions; and admission and discharge planning were delineated. The focus of this report will be the *seriously ill chronic psychotic patient* who may suffer from problems within any of the above descriptive groupings. The report will demonstrate that the public hospital providing longterm care has a necessary and significant role to play in the provision of the spectrum of services chronic psychotic mental patients require.

We have chosen to discuss the work of public sector hospitals rather than that of private facilities, because the vast majority of chronically psychotic patients are treated in the public sector.[13] We believe, nevertheless, that the private hospital plays an important role in longterm care. In a subsequent report we shall turn attention to the significant role of longterm hospitalization for the psychodynamic treatment of the chronic mental patient. The focus on longterm hospitalization should not be misconstrued as an attack on the positive aspects of outpatient treatment which have been demonstrated. The fact remains, however, that there is still much to be understood about what constitutes "optimal" treatment for our seriously ill chronic psychiatric populations.

The concept, the process and the reality of deinstitutionalization has continued to be surrounded by a storm of controversy with much rhetoric as to both the positive and negative aspects of this movement. There is no question that the deinstitutionalization movement was in part a response to legitimate concerns about the quality of care for chronic mental patients. Recent data indicate that the move to community-based treatment of chronic psychiatric patients has gone too far, too quickly, with too little planning and preparation. The case is not as clear as has been stated that the elimination of hospitals providing longterm treatment, which are primarily state and county hospitals, is either a wise or beneficial decision. This is not to ignore the abuses that have occurred within the state hospital system or to call for a return to previous transgressions. Nor is it to say that the deinstitutionalization movement has been without benefit. But to decide from these considerations that all longterm hospitalization is bad and should be eliminated would leave a certain proportion of our chronic mental patients without the locus of care for them to obtain needed, appropriate, and adequate treatment. The social struggle of how best to deal with a chronic psychiatric population that "refuses to go away" would be made more, rather than less, difficult by dismantling the longterm public hospital system.

The chronic care system for psychiatric patients is a system in transition. Local communities as well as the private sector have taken on some of the responsibility and burden of care for this population. Nonetheless, while it may be theoretically possible for most of the chronic care system to take place within communities, in reality, satisfactory alternatives for most patients with chronic mental illness have not been provided. There is little evidence that better alternatives in the community will ever become a reality.

There have been a number of definitions of the chronic mental patient.[13, 41, 42, 45] Peele (personal communication) has defined the chronic mental patient as a "person who needs psychiatric services indefinitely to attain and preserve the maximum possible independence from a substantially disabling mental illness." In this report we shall focus our attention on those patients, with a diagnosis of *psychosis*, with severe disability in social and vocational role functioning, and with a duration of illness of at least two years. While some will argue with the

breadth or narrowness of the definition, most can agree that
there is a hard core of such chronic patients that are not
appropriate for *most* community-based programs. Kraft et al[43]
estimated their number at 1 percent of hospitalized patients. In
Switzerland, where social supports for the mentally ill are im-
pressive, Bleuler[44] estimated that at least 10 percent of schizo-
phrenics should remain permanently hospitalized.

Several clinical examples of chronic patients who need and/or
could benefit from longterm hospitalization may better illustrate
the population of concern:

- A 38-year-old single man has a 20-year history of 25
  psychiatric hospitalizations (more than 13 years of hospital
  stay) for recurrent psychotic decompensations in a malig-
  nant chronic psychotic process. A pattern of leaving his
  sheltered residence, inappropriately spending his social
  security allotment, self-neglect, erratic attendance at his
  day program and medication clinic remains unmodifiable.
- A 27-year-old single man with repeated hospitalizations
  for assaultive behavior based on a chronic paranoid de-
  lusional system remains unresponsive to current medications.
- A 25-year-old single woman with a 10-year history of
  persistent unremitting psychosis, unresponsive to current
  treatment interventions, is repeatedly sexually abused when
  living outside a structured environment in the community.
  She refuses to attend any structured day or evening program, and manages escape from a locked skilled nursing
  home.
- A 40-year-old chronically psychotic man with a long history
  of alcohol abuse, deinstitutionalized after 15 years of
  hospitalization and relative sobriety, has many readmis-
  sions for serious alcohol abuse and psychotic decompensations. He refuses all attempts at alcohol treatment.
- A 65-year-old woman diagnosed as chronic, undifferenti-

ated schizophrenic has increasing loss of cognitive ability. She is no longer able to live independently or receive adequate support in the day hospital setting she has been attending. She repeatedly wanders away from each nursing home in which she is placed, as well as being unpredictably combative within the nursing home.

The state hospital is the institution that has historically contained these kinds of patients. Despite our best efforts and intentions, the public sector hospital system will probably continue as the final answer—the locus of care—for those patients for whom no other agency cares. In response to the question, "What are we going to do with these patients in the future?" it seems likely that longterm, in addition to short-term, hospitalization and institutionalization is useful for the seriously ill chronic psychiatric patients who need it. We maintain that there will always be a need for institutional-based (public sector) treatment facilities.

2

POSITIVE ASPECTS OF LONGTERM HOSPITALIZATION

Let us now focus on the positive aspects of longterm hospitalization which we group within six general areas:

- Structure, containment, and support
- Total care: comprehensiveness of services
- Relief for the community and family
- Asylum
- Clarification of diagnostic problems and evaluation of treatment response
- Research

We shall then discuss the implications of these aspects for the longterm treatment of chronic mental patients.

Structure, Containment, and Support

The hospital providing longterm care like most hospitals, can provide a controlled, stable environment for disturbed patients without undue stimulation. It is a place in which there is authority, usually medical authority, and shared responsibility among a hierarchy of staff for the treatment of such patients.

The concept of *structure* has yet to be systematically developed and explored. It seems to refer to an important complex of external interactions which help the disordered person to order his internal life and pattern his everyday behaviors. Gunderson[46] has defined structure as "all aspects of a milieu which provide a predictable organization of time, place, and person." (p. 331) Structure refers to the predictability, consistency, order, and organization of all the environment. The structural aspects of the hospital can provide containment for the out-of-control, protection for the unprotected, and support and nurturance for the unwanted.

For the chronic mental patient, longterm hospitalization can provide a stable environment in which the level of stimulation can be regulated. Those aspects of structure which the facility may use to compensate for disorganization include many of the services which are conventionally called custodial. Awakening and sleep times are determined, baths can be given, meals prepared, clothes bought, and exercises organized. Cues for appropriate behaviors can also be provided by staff, in the form of reminders to make one's bed, come to meals, take one's medications, and attend to one's attire. Thus patients who are insufficiently able to order their lives to meet their basic needs are able to benefit from the care which others can directly provide in meeting those needs within a normalizing structure. Such structuring requires an adequate number of trained staff.

Gunderson identifies the function of *containment* as sustaining the "physical well-being of patients and removing the unaccepted burdens of self control" (pp. 328–9). The chronically mentally ill are frequently troubled by disabling degrees of disorganized thinking, even when properly medicated. Their perceptual and associative apparatus may be so distorted and poorly functioning that they are unable to process even the simplest of everyday tasks and respond in a self-protective or socially appropriate fashion.

There are also patients who need special types of structure to help control unpredictable, sometimes violent, impulses. The assaultive patient, the self-destructive patient, the patient who touches impulsively or exposes himself, are often unable to control their own behavior sufficiently to avoid social disturbance, public outrage, or legal action. The patient whose behavior is so extreme, needs support, and containment and protection from his/her own social inappropriateness. The self-destructive patient needs external help to shield him from his own harsh self-treatment. Self-destructive behavior may not be eliminated within the time constraints of acute psychiatric hospital treatment. Suicidal feelings and ideation may be chronic problems for some patients. While many of these people can manage in the community or at levels of care less intensive than a hospital, for some, only easy and rapid access to protective caretakers will suffice. For these unfortunate people the degree of containment can mean the difference between wholeness and mutilation, life and death.

Structure can also help the chronic psychotic patient learn new patterns for adaptive living. Because the ability to appreciate means-ends relationships deteriorates in chronic mental illness, the repetition of new, more adaptive behaviors can result in enhanced learning and ability to function. Because of the limited ability of certain patients to retain learned behavior, therapeutic contacts on a monthly, weekly, or even daily basis may not suffice for rehabilitation. Continual monitoring and structuring of expected behavior can be a benefit of hospitalization which lower level of care facilities cannot easily match.

Structure, containment, and support are the products of those services which the hospital can provide to either compensate for the patient's disorganization or to help the patient organize his thoughts and impulses at a higher level of functioning. Theoretically such structure could and should be provided within smaller units within the community (i.e., in sheltered living situations). In reality, however, the longterm hospital remains the only place outside the penal system that provides such structure.

Total Care: Comprehensiveness of Services

The hospital providing longterm care can offer a comprehensive system of services: psychiatric, medical and dental, aftercare planning and support that may not be readily available in the community, especially for the chronic mental patient.[39] In the best of our model community programs, coordination of necessary services may exist. However, most chronic mental patients do not have the internal or external resources to obtain diverse social, welfare, and medical services that may be available, unless they are directly provided to them.[47]

In addition, a variety of specific reparative social skills training can be instituted within the hospital including interpersonal skills training, recreational activities, development of avocations, prevocational and vocational skills training, problem solving, educational skills, and day-to-day living skills. However, it does remain unproven that social skills training in the hospital generalizes in any way to performance in the community.

Behavior modification, group confrontation and other programs for controlling anti-social and asocial behavior can be instituted. Team work among staff can create particular situations, leading to consistency of interpersonal response. Group pressure can mobilize individuals. Behavior modification can mold more adaptive responses and decrease maladaptive ones. Medication can be regulated over a long period of time. Other somatic treatments such as electroconvulsive therapy (ECT) can be provided. Continuing observation of patients with accurate 24-hour feedback and monitoring of information can be provided. Families can be offered support, education, and assistance in dealing with their disturbed members; though, again, the physical isolation of such institutions has often made family participation relatively unworkable. In sum, the hospital allows for a centralization and coordination of services, a total co-ordinated treatment approach, as well as a place of staff commitment and staff expertise.

Relief for the Community and Family

Hospitalization can provide relief for the community from a situation(s) which has become impossible for either patient, family, or neighbors, by removing the patient from his/her usual environment.[33]

Work in this area often earns the gratitude of the community. Respite may be temporary, or more permanent. For some chronic patients, longer periods of hospitalization may give the community longer relief from the individual, and allow for some adjustments within the environment to improve the chances for adaptation of patient and community. There is an implied extended but nonetheless time limitation to the course of hospitalization. For others, indefinite hospitalization may be necessary.

As part of such care, longterm hospitalization may provide the chronic mentally ill individual and the community with an alternative to the legal system. Longer term hospitalization can give the patient's family relief from excessive demands and complaints from the hostile, paranoid, or abusive patient. It can provide an atmosphere to help the patient and family reorient their relationships to a perhaps more helpful perspective. It can support a family by allowing periodic "vacations" from the patient. It can help protect society from dangerous individuals.[29, 43, 48]

Asylum

By asylum we mean the safety which a hospital can offer to a group of patients unable to shield themselves from basic adversities. Such people may require feeding to prevent malnourishment and sheltering to prevent exposure. Lacking protection in a period of disorganization, they may become targets of violence or exploitation.

Beyond protection, a hospital can offer acceptance and comfort. At its best, it is a place where a patient can expect to be treated with caring and kindness, despite severely disturbed behavior. For the chronic patient the hospital may resemble a home, with its familiar environment and inhabitants. Perhaps it should be considered the most fitting place for some individuals to live, an attitude which would suggest in some cases reducing the obstacles to admission. For some chronic mental patients, the hospital is the place where one cannot be too sick, where one can live indefinitely in a refuge from a world that is overwhelming.

A number of chronic mental patients return to the hospital

because of distress or deterioration in functioning. Others may return because of a lack of available alternatives, such as the absence or unavailability of family and support groups, or a lack of adequate minimal community resources. For still others who return, the reasons seem to relate to not wanting to leave the asylum in the first place. A large number of patients who benefit from longterm hospitalization would voluntarily choose to remain hospitalized if they could.[53, 58] These patients perhaps accurately assess their impaired capacity to adapt in the community and choose to remain within the safe and supportive confines of the hospital. The needs of this group of patients should be respected and longterm care made available in a safe, caring asylum. For some chronic patients, the public hospital is the location which is "least restrictive" among the patient's options.[8, 49–57]

Clarification of Diagnostic Problems and Evaluation of Treatment Response

Acute psychiatric hospitalization has as its goal the rapid evaluation and treatment of individuals so they may be returned to the community for continued treatment. Short-term psychiatric hospitalization however is often inadequate to undertake intensive innovative treatments in seriously ill chronic psychiatric patients.[39, 58, 59] Longterm hospitalization, beyond six months, allows for diagnostic and therapeutic evaluation through twenty-four-hour-a-day observation, drug-free, and intensive psychological and biological workup by a skilled professional staff. Removing people from their environmental stressors gives a new perspective to individual strengths and deficits, permitting careful and multidisciplinary observation of response to various treatments.[39] It may also partially obscure the natural course of the disorder.

Longterm psychiatric hospitalization allows for more successful pharmacologic treatment, monitoring of blood levels and side-effects, switching if necessary to new drugs which may best be initiated in an inpatient facility. Such hospitalization may allow for the undertaking of intensive psychodynamic treatment. Longterm hospitalization may even begin the process of skills training and community reorientation for chronic psychotic patients within specialized behavioral and rehabilitative wards.[39]

One of the major problems faced by psychiatric hospitals providing longterm care has been their isolation (physical and otherwise) from medical centers and their professional and technologic resources.

Research

As long as an understanding of both the etiologies and the effective and appropriate treatment methodologies for chronic psychiatric disorders remain inadequate, there will be the need for locations to carry out continuing investigations. The long-term public sector hospital can and should serve as a place to continue work in the understanding of the phenomenology of disease, the close monitoring of disease course, the development of new treatments, and the application of new treatment methodologies.[60] Such research belongs with the population of interest and should be carried on within such hospitals. The traditional isolation of public hospitals from medical centers must be corrected. It should be clear, however, that no patient should be kept in a hospital for extended periods of time solely for research purposes. Finally, safeguards need to be instituted to protect patients' rights as well as to ensure informed consent.

3

DISCUSSION

Through each cycle of reform we, as a nation, come close to providing adequate resources for minimal humane care of the chronic mentally ill, and then for a variety of social, economic, philosophical and other reasons withdraw. As a society we seem unable to accept the reality of people who "do not get better," who cannot manage unprotected within our society. The reality remains that with all the competing societal priorities, we are unwilling to spend the necessary resources on the chronic mentally ill.

A large and ever expanding literature has developed discussing all aspects of what has become known as the deinstitutionalization movement and community care of the chronic mental patient.[4, 8, 11, 14, 22–24, 26, 27, 31, 33, 41, 47, 54, 55, 58, 61–79] Effective and appropriate care for chronic mental patients depends on a careful, realistic definition of the individuals to be served, the nature of the services they need, as well as the "communities" in which they are to be treated. The treatment of these patients has become intertwined with what has become known as the deinstitutionalization movement. In addition to those patients that have been deinstitutionalized, there are at least four other groups of chronic patients: the revolving door short-stay patient, the continuously institutionalized long-stay chronic patient, the newly institutionalized long-stay chronic patient, and the chronic patient who has never been hospitalized.[58, 67, 69, 79]

The fundamental care problems of all these groups have more similarities than differences. Bachrach[22, 41, 47] defines deinstitutionalization as (1) the eschewal of traditional institutional settings, primarily state hospitals, for the care of the mentally ill,

17

and (2) the concurrent expansion of community-based services for the treatment of these individuals. Bachrach sees the deinstitutionalization movement as the expression of a philosophy current in American thought; a philosophy that places strong, civil-libertarian emphasis on the rights of the individual and on modification of the environment as the primary avenue to social change, including the care of the mentally ill. According to Bachrach, the philosophy of deinstitutionalization involves three fundamental assumptions: (1) that community mental health and community-based care are preferable to institutional care for most if not all mental patients; (2) that communities not only can but are willing to assume responsibility and leadership in the care of the mentally ill; and (3) that the functions performed by the hospital can be performed equally well if not better by community-based facilities (i.e., the community is capable of providing a full range of patient services that were traditionally available within the hospital).

Many of the problems confronting the deinstitutionalization movement and the treatment of chronic mental patients may result from the failure to provide such functional alternatives for some of the basic functions served by the mental hospital. Deinstitutionalization was and is still too often viewed as an end in itself. Many have felt that placing chronic patients within a community setting would result in their "getting better." [33, 41, 62, 63, 70, 74, 75, 79] However, a wide range of services and facilities are needed to care for the fragmented groups of chronic mental patients in the community. These services which include residential, crisis intervention, financial, dietary, medical, rehabilitative, social, to name but a few, are generally unavailable within the community except in a few model programs. [47] When available the skills to manage such diverse services are often beyond the resources of the chronic mentally ill person. The development of a social system network in the community may be very difficult. When one asks the question, "What would be necessary to provide to the chronic mental patient in the community those necessary functions in a reliable, available, fashion?'', one obvious answer is an institution which would provide longterm care.

Not only are chronic mental patients a fragmented group in need of diverse services, but the assumption that the community is a less restrictive treatment alternative may be fallacious. Is the board and care, or nursing home in an inner city ghetto really less restrictive than the old state hospital? Is it less restrictive to continually fear for one's safety, and the potential loss of one's meager financial resources? Are patients freer when what is expected of them may be unrealistic? Bachrach[80] has argued forcefully for a careful look at the multivariate nature of restrictiveness. Residence is not the only criterion of restrictiveness. Whether in the community or in the hospital, the issue should not be the locus of care, but which functions must be provided in working with chronic mental patients. The hospital providing longterm care may be a more successful location, that is, perhaps no more restrictive a place, to perform such functions for certain patients.

For the most severely disturbed chronic patients one must ask what has happened in the community as compared to the institutional alternative. Despite the dramatic drop in numbers of patients in state hospitals, Goldman et al[13] estimate that about 1 percent of the United States population, between 1.7 and 2.4 million people, are chronic mental patients. Ten percent of those (170,000) are within state and county hospitals; another 40 percent reside in nursing homes. Further, the percent of our citizens who live in institutions has not significantly changed in the recent past.[9]

The current choice seems to lie between poorly financed hospital care and poorly financed community care. While one can estimate the cost of caring for patients in the hospital, costs become so diffuse in the community that there is almost no way to compare the two. The assumption that costs are less in the community certainly remains unproven. In part, the cost of caring for a patient in the community will be dependent on the amount of services the patient needs.

The question remains unresolved as to where that money should be spent. Perhaps the more basic question is how can the severely ill chronic mental patient best be served. It is clear that society has some difficult and perhaps impossible choices, but it must choose. Development of community mental health facilities is beneficial when it widens the diversity of treatment options for chronic mental patients, not when it closes options. Realistically, it does not seem possible that all of the functions of a longterm public hospital can be replaced by any combination of even adequately financed community services. Attempts are likely to prove more costly, and not necessarily less institutional. Test and Stein demonstrate that the cost of treating chronic mental patients is very high if adequate care is to be given.[78] Hospitals providing longterm care are a necessary *part* of a comprehensive treatment system.[58, 60] One cannot, however, be satisfied with the current public mental hospitals' inability to carry out the overabundance of functions assigned to them with inadequate staffing levels, overbureaucratization, and antiquated, isolated physical plants.

Lack of adequate planning, oversimplification, denial of needs, as well as the diverse range of necessary services all remind us that the movement to close longterm public hospitals and deinstitutionalize their clientele has fallen far short of its goals.[8, 14, 17–19, 27, 58, 63, 64, 74, 76, 79, 81] Test and Stein[78] have demonstrated that modest gains can be achieved through direct, intense, *in situ* intervention with chronic patients. These gains can only be sustained as long as treatment continues. Such model programs are too small in number, and probably too expensive to suffice as a solution. In addition, what works in such programs may not be generalizable for large scale application.[47]

The community mental health center movement has been unable to replace the state hospital system. Among the reasons include inadequate funding, as well as the political developments that withdrew support before the deficiencies of the original plan and the conceptual errors could be corrected. In addition, state governments, in part, used the movement as a means of closing costly state institutions. Attempts to coordinate care through a system of case managers seems largely to have added an additional and ineffective layer of bureaucracy.[82] Particularly, given the financial realities[64] one sees little evidence that the private sector is willing to adequately assume the burden for the functions of longterm hospital care for chronic psychotic patients except in model programs. Plans for the operation of all services through contractual arrangements with the private sector, while having some merit, remain theoretical. Given how little the private sector has done, it does not seem likely that they will provide adequate facilities of last resort. One must hope the notorious case of the nursing home industry is not such an example. This is not to say that the private sector has no role to play, especially in the psychodynamic treatment of such patients and their families. As stated before, however, this is the subject of another report.

Rachlin et al[54] have emphasized that it is the severely ill and the chronically ill who are most in need of the services provided by the public hospital. The public hospital, past and present, functions within a service delivery system providing care to some patients that no other segment has yet accepted with adequate responsibility—"the referral of last resort that accepts the patient for care or treatment based only on his needs"[83] (p. 39).

We have described the functions of the public hospital providing longterm care, both in what it really does and what it should be doing. The most salient criticism of the state hospital system is that "it has not worked in the past." An effective public sector hospital system providing longterm care is a necessary part of the system of psychiatric services for severely disabled mental patients. While such hospitals *can* provide such services, whether they *will* remains an unanswered question hinging largely on financial considerations.

How to organize such hospitals remains a complex problem. It is necessary to replace the present deteriorated physical plants with modern treatment facilities of appropriate size and architectural design, located in population centers close to and affiliated with other major medical facilities if the system is to successfully provide the longterm care chronic mental patients deserve and require. A good public hospital will attract more referrals than it can handle. It must remain relatively small (less than 200 beds[84]) to maintain quality. It must not become a self-contained, isolated institution without freedom of movement for patients across its boundaries into and out of the community. The community must maintain an ongoing involvement and accountability monitor function. Attention to the special aspects of longterm care, inservice training, and manpower development, in addition, can make such work more rewarding for staff personnel at all levels.

How broad a scope of functions a good longterm hospital should provide remains a question. While the longterm hospital cannot and should not exist in isolation from the larger mental health system, what tertiary care functions it should provide need further clarification. Miller[60] and Barter[83] see the longterm hospital system as providing back-up facilities for patients who cannot be treated in community settings. But to what degree do these institutions then attempt to become acute treatment units? How many specialized services for special difficult patient groups (i.e., the addictions) should be provided, with the danger of diluting the primary mission of the care of the chronic mental patient? How much professional training and research can be provided without diverting attention to more "interesting" problems? How does one offer community liaison without inherently devaluing the tasks of the longterm institution? While these and many other questions remain unsolved, the primary mission of the hospital providing longterm care must encompass the functions we have reviewed: structure and containment, total care, and asylum for chronic mental patients. It must not be distracted into either an acute care or ambulatory care mission which can only dilute its focus.

A final supposition that requires questioning is the belief that the syndrome of "institutionalism" is a function of institutionalization per se. Institutionalism may be a consequence of neglect and depersonalization in any setting including the community.[33, 35, 79, 85] For certain subgroups of patients, it may be an irremediable aspect of the course of their illnesses. Institutional treatment does not necessarily have to have a pernicious deteriorating effect on the personality of chronic patients if attention is given to appropriate size, staffing pattern, therapeutic environment, and the like.

Furthermore, treatment in a longterm institution does not inherently constitute abridgment of fundamental civil rights.[27] Longterm care has been drastically modified by economic and legal realities. The laws governing hospitalization vary, and, in some states, make longterm hospitalization difficult or impossible. The reasoning behind the various state laws that have shortened involuntary hospitalization, as well as the economic and administrative pressures against longterm voluntary hospitalization, has not adequately taken into account the positive aspects of longterm hospital care. It is time to reexamine the laws in light of what is in the patients' clinical interests.

On all levels—professional, public, and political—we must continue to address the deplorable conditions that exist in the care of treating chronically ill mental patients. Humanitarian ends cannot be achieved by closing all longterm hospitals any more than they can be achieved by less costly care. There needs to be high quality care available in both the community and in hospitals for longterm care so that individual patients can receive the care they need and deserve.[74, 86] If society is unwilling to make the necessary commitment, then it can hardly blame the longterm care system (whether it be primarily in the community, in the institution, or with a combined effort) for its failure. Ideally, perhaps, the private sector might be able to work with or run the public hospital system through some contractual mechanism better than the current governmental arrangements. The problem of financial commitment, nonetheless, remains more the issue than the locus of care. As mental health professionals, we must not accept inadequate care in either the community or longterm care facility. It seems likely that it is only a matter of time before the mental hospital providing longterm care is "rediscovered."

4

RECOMMENDATIONS

We live with all types of institutions in our society. It is our belief that the time has come to reassess the notion that institutions are inherently bad. Social policy necessarily requires plans based on beliefs, at times with conflicting value systems regarding the nature of social realities. We wish to enumerate the following principles about the role of the public sector hospital providing longterm care in a balanced system of delivery of mental health services.

- Every community needs a comprehensive spectrum of psychiatric services based on the needs of patients. The public hospital providing longterm care is an essential component within that spectrum of services.
- There is a significant number of chronic patients who are unable to function independently in the community. The longterm public hospital at present is the most appropriate place for such patients to receive the kinds of services they need.
- For some chronic patients, the public hospital may provide the least restrictive environment and should be the place in which such patients live and receive treatment.
- While community-based care may be preferable for many patients, longterm hospitalization may be more appropriate for some chronic mental patients because of humane, therapeutic, and perhaps economic reasons. The hospital may provide the structure, containment, support and asylum that some patients seek.
- Efforts should be directed towards ensuring the highest level of care possible in longterm institutions.

- The search for newer therapeutic methods should continue in multiple settings. The longterm hospital provides a unique opportunity for intensive, innovative diagnostic and research efforts. The public hospital offering longterm care can provide a setting in which learning, growth, and habilitation may be accomplished by patients when all else has failed.
- These principles should be a part of all community health care planning.

REFERENCES

1. G. W. Albee. Psychiatry's Human Resources: 20 Years Later, *Hospital and Community Psychiatry* 30,11 (1979) 783–786.
2. D. Bennett. Community Psychiatry, *British Journal of Psychiatry* 132, (1978) 209–229.
3. A. Deutsch. THE SHAME OF THE STATES (New York: Harcourt, Brace 1948).
4. Group for the Advancement of Psychiatry. THE CHRONIC MENTAL PATIENT IN THE COMMUNITY. GAP Report No. 102 (New York: GAP, May 1978).
5. E. Goffman, ASYLUMS (New York: Anchor Books 1961).
6. M. Greenblatt and E. Glazier. The Phasing Out of Mental Hospitals in the United States, *American Journal of Psychiatry* 132,11 (1975) 1135–1140.
7. R. F. Mollica and F. Redlich. Equity and Changing Patient Characteristics 1950–1975, *Archives of General Psychiatry* 37 (1980) 1257–1263.
8. J. P. Morrisey, H. H. Goldman, and L. V. Klerman. THE ENDURING ASYLUM: *Cycles of Institutional Reform at Worcester State Hospital* (New York: Grune and Stratton, 1980).
9. D. F. Musto. Whatever Happened to Community Mental Health? *Psychiatric Annals* 7,10 (1977) 30–55.
10. F. Redlich and S. R. Kellert. Trends in American Mental Health, *American Journal of Psychiatry* 135,1 (178) 22–28.
11. J. A. Talbott. STATE MENTAL HOSPITALS (New York: Human Sciences Press, 1980).
12. I. M. Greenberg. "The Problems of State Hospitals," in STATE MENTAL HOSPITALS, J. A. Talbott, ed. (New York: Human Sciences Press, 1980). Chapter 2, pp. 33–46.
13. H. H. Goldman, A. A. Gattozzi, and C. A. Taube. Defining and

Counting the Chronically Mentally Ill, *Hospital and Community Psychiatry* 32,1 (1981) 21–27.

14. H. R. Lamb. What Did We Really Expect From Deinstitutionalization. *Hospital and Community Psychiatry* 32,2 (1981) 105–109.

15. H. Goldman, C. Taube and D. Regier. *The Present and Future Role of the State Mental Hospital* (Rockville, Md.: National Institute of Mental Health, Division of Biometry and Epidemiology, 1979).

16. ACTION FOR MENTAL HEALTH: *The Final Report of the Joint Commission on Mental Illness and Health* (New York: Basic Books, 1961).

17. Report to the Congress by the Controller General of the United States. Returning the Mentally Disabled to the Community: Government Needs to Do More. (Washington, D.C.: Department of Health, Education and Welfare, 1977.) Publication No. (HRD) 76-152.

18. C. Windle and D. Scully. Community Mental Health Centers and The Decreasing Use of State Mental Hospitals, *Community Mental Health Journal* 12 (1976) 239–243.

19. HEW Task Force on the Report to the President from the President's Commission on Mental Health. (Washington, D.C.: Department of Health, Education and Welfare, 1979.) Publication No. (Adm.) 79-848.

20. D. Aanes, and J. Wills. The Impact of a Community Hospital's Psychiatric Unit on a Regional State Hospital, *Hospital and Community Psychiatry* 26,9 (1975) 596–598.

21. R. I. Almed and S. C. Plog, ed. STATE MENTAL HOSPITALS: WHAT HAPPENS WHEN THEY CLOSE (New York: Plenum Press, 1976).

22. L. L. Bachrach. A Conceptual Approach to Deinstitutionalization *Hospital and Community Psychiatry* 29,9 (1978) 573–577.

23. J. T. Barter. Sacramento County's Experience With Community Care. *Hospital and Community Psychiatry* 26,9 (1975) 587–589.

24. A Becker and H. C. Schulberg. Phasing Out State Hospitals—A Psychiatric Dilemma, *The New England Journal of Medicine* 294,5 (1976) 255–261.

25. E. M. Bonn. The Impact of Redeployment of Funds on a Model State Hospital, *Hospital and Community Psychiatry* 26,9 (1975) 584–586.

26. J. R. Elpers. Orange County's Alternative to State Hospital Treatment, *Hospital and Community Psychiatry* 26,9 (1975) 589–592.

27. E. M. Gruenberg and J. Archer. Abandonment of Responsibility for the Seriously Mentally Ill, *Milbank Memorial Fund Quarterly* 57,4 (1979) 485–506.

28. D. K. Kentsmith, W. W. Menninger, and L. Coyne. A Survey of State Hospital Admissions From an Area Served by a Mental Health Center, *Hospital and Community Psychiatry* 26,9 (1975) 593–598.

29. H. R. Lamb and V. Goertzel. The Demise of the State Hospital—A Premature Obituary? *Archives of General Psychiatry* 26 (1972) 489–495.

30. M. P. Lawton, M. B. Lipton, M. C. Fulcomer, and M. H. Kleban. Planning for a Mental Hospital Phasedown, *American Journal of Psychiatry* 134:12 (1977) 1386–1390.

31. D. G. Langlsey and J. T. Barter. Treatment in the Community or State Hospital: An Evaluation, *Psychiatric Annals* 5,5 (1975) 163–170.

32. L. D. Ozarin and A. T. Leverson. The Future of the Public Mental Hospital, *American Journal of Psychiatry* 125 (1969) 1647–1652.

33. W. R. Shadish and R. R. Bootzin. Nursing Homes and the Chronic Mental Patients, *Schizophrenia Bulletin* 7,3 (1981) 488–498.

34. M. Sills. The Transfer of State Hospital Resources to Community Programs, *Hospital and Community Psychiatry* 26,9 (1975) 577–581.

35. D. C. Smith, T. A. Jones and J. L. Coyle. State Mental Health Institutions in the Next Decade: Illusions and Reality, *Hospital and Community Psychiatry* 28,8 (1977) 593–597.

36. N. E. Stratas, D. B. Bernhart, and R. N. Elwell. The Future of the State Mental Hospital: Developing a Unified System of Care, *Hospital and Community Psychiatry* 28,4 (1977) 598–600.

37. J. K. Wing and G. W. Brown. INSTITUTIONALISM AND SCHIZO-PHRENIA (Cambridge: Cambridge University Press, 1970).

38. J. Zusman, A. Bertsch, editors. THE FUTURE ROLE OF THE STATE HOSPITAL (Lexington, Mass.: Heath, 1975). (Especially: H. W. Demone and H. C. Schulberg. "Has the State Hospital a Future as a Human Service Resource," pp. 9–29).

39. Group for the Advancement of Psychiatry. CRISIS IN PSYCHIATRIC HOSPITALIZATION. GAP Report No. 72 (New York: GAP, March, 1969).

40. M. Herz. Short Term Hospitalization and the Medical Model, *Hospital and Community Psychiatry* 30 (1979) 117–121.

41. L. L. Bachrach. DEINSTITUTIONALIZATION: AN ANALYTICAL REVIEW AND SOCIOLOGICAL PERSPECTIVE (Washington, D.C.: NIMH, 1976).

42. K. Minoff. "A Map of Chronic Mental Patients." In THE CHRONIC MENTAL PATIENT, J. A. Talbott, ed. (Washington, D.C.: American Psychiatric Association, 1979) pp. 11–37.

43. A. M. Kraft, P. R. Binner, and B. A. Dickey. The Community Mental Health Program and the Longer Stay Patient, *Archives of General Psychiatry* 16 (1967) 64–70.

44. M. Bleuler. Second Rochester International Conference on Schizophrenia. Reported in *Frontiers in Psychiatry* 6,17 (1976).

45. H. Brill. "State Hospitals Should Be Kept for How Long? In STATE MENTAL HOSPITALS, J. A. Talbott, ed. (New York: Human Sciences Press, 1980).

46. J. Gunderson. Defining the Therapeutic Process in Psychiatric Milieus, *Psychiatry* 41 (1978) 327–335.

47. L. L. Bachrach. Overview: Model Programs for Chronic Mental Patients, *American Journal of Psychiatry* 137,9 (1980) 1023–1031.

48. H. R. Lamb. The State Hospital: Facility of Last Resort. *American Journal of Psychiatry* 134 (1977) 1151–1152.

49. R. E. Drake and M. A. Wallach. Will Mental Patients Stay in the Community? A Social Psychological Perspective, *Journal of Consulting and Clinical Psychology* 47,2 (1979) 285–294.

50. D. F. Spiegel and P. Keith-Spiegal. Why We Came Back: A Study of Patients Readmitted to a Mental Hospital, *Mental Hygiene* 53,3 (1969) 433–437.

51. D. Birnbach. Back Ward Society, 1981: Implications for Residential Treatment and Staff Training, *Hospital and Community Psychiatry* 32,8 (1981) 550–555.

52. B. Cochran. Where Is My Home? The Closing of State Mental Hospitals, *Hospital and Community Psychiatry* 25,6 (1974) 393–401.

53. E. M. Kinard. Discharged Patients' Attitudes Toward Hospital Staff, *Hospital and Community Psychiatry* 32,3 (1981) 194–197.

54. S. Rachlin, S. Grossman, and J. Frankel. Patients Without Communities: Whose Responsibility? *Hospital and Community Psychiatry* 30,1 (1979) 37–40.

55. E. Robbins and L. Robbins. Charge to the Community: Some Early Effects of a State Hospital System's Change of Policy, *American Journal of Psychiatry* 131,6 (1974) 641–644.

56. A. Rosenblatt. Providing Custodial Care for Mental Patients: An Affirmative View, *Psychiatric Quarterly* 48,1 (1974) 14–25.
57. R. M. Weinstein. Mental Patients' Attitudes Toward Hospital Staff. *Archives of General Psychiatry* 38,4 (1981) 483–487.
58. L. L. Bachrach. Planning Mental Health Services for Chronic Patients, *Hospital and Community Psychiatry* 30,6 (1979) 387–392.
59. C. J. Rabiner and E. Lurie. The Case for Psychiatric Hospitalization, *American Journal of Psychiatry* 131 (1974) 761–764.
60. R. D. Miller. Beyond the Old State Hospital: New Opportunities Ahead, *Hospital and Community Psychiatry* 32,1 (1981) 27–31.
61. APA Position Statement on the Need to Maintain Long Term Mental Hospital Facilities, *American Journal of Psychiatry* 131,6 (1974) 745.
62. J. W. Ashbaugh and V. J. Bradley. Linking Deinstitutionalization of Patients with Hospital Phase-Down: The Difference Between Success and Failure *Hospital and Community Psychiatry* 30,2 (1979) 105–110.
63. E. L. Bassuk and S. Gerson. Deinstitutionalization and Mental Health Services, *Scientific American* 238,2 (1978) 46–53.
64. J. Borus. Deinstitutionalization of the Chronically Mentally Ill, *New England Journal of Medicine* 305 (1981) 339–342.
65. P. Braun, G. Kochansky, et al. Overview: Deinstitutionalization of Psychiatric Patients, A Critical Review of Outcome Studies, *American Journal of Psychiatry* 138,6 (1981) 736–749.
66. G. J. Clarke. In Defense of Deinstitutionalization. *Milbank Memorial Fund Quarterly* 57,4 (1979) 461–479.
67. R. A. Dorwart. Deinstitutionalization: Who is Left Behind? *Hospital and Community Psychiatry* 31,5 (1980) 336–338.
68. H. R. Lamb. The New Asylums in the Community. *Archives of General Psychiatry* 36 (1979) 129–134.
69. H. R. Lamb. Roots of Neglect of the Long-term Mentally Ill, *Psychiatry* 42 (1979) 201–207.
70. H. R. Lamb. Structure: The Neglected Ingredient of Community Treatment, *Archives of General Psychiatry* 37 (1980) 1224–1228.
71. S. M. Rose. Deciphering Deinstitutionalization: Complexities in Policy and Program Analysis. *Milbank Memorial Fund Quarterly* 51,4 (1979) 429–460.
72. D. J. Scherl and L. B. Macht. Deinstitutionalization in the Absence

of Consensus, *Hospital and Community Psychiatry* 30,9 (1979) 599–604.

73. S. P. Segal. Community Care and Deinstitutionalization: A Review, *Social Work* (1979) 521–527.

74. Department of Health and Human Services Steering Committee on the Chronically Mentally Ill. (Washington, D.C.: DHHS December 1980). Publication No. (Adm) 81-1077.

75. W. G. Smith and D. W. Hart. Community Mental Health: A Noble Failure? *Hospital and Community Psychiatry* 26,9 (1975) 581–583.

76. J. A. Talbott. Deinstitutionalization: Avoiding the Disasters of the Past, *Hospital and Community Psychiatry* 30,9 (1979) 621–624.

77. J. A. Talbott, J. K. Wing and R. Olsen. COMMUNITY CARE OF THE MENTALLY DISABLED (New York: Oxford University Press, 1979).

78. M. A. Test and L. I. Stein. Community Treatment of the Chronic Patient: Research Overview, *Schizophrenia Bulletin* 4,3 (1978) 350–364.

79. J. K. Wing. From Institutional to Community Care, *Psychiatric Quarterly* 53,2 (1981).

80. L. L .Bachrach. Is the Least Restrictive Environment Always the Best? Sociological and Semantic Implications, *Hospital and Community Psychiatry* 31,2 (1980) 97–103.

81. "Report of the Task Panel on Deinstitutionalization, Rehabilitation, and Longterm Care." In TASK PANEL REPORTS, submitted to the President's Commission on Mental Health. Vol. 2 (Washington, D.C.: NIMH 1978) pp. 356–375.

82. W. S. Deitchman. How Many Case Managers Does It Take To Screw in A Lightbulb? *Hospital and Community Psychiatry* 31,11 (1980) 788–789.

83. J. Barter. "State Hospitals as Tertiary Care Facilities. In STATE MENTAL HOSPITALS, J. A. Talbot, ed. (New York: Human Sciences Press, 1980). Chapter 10, pp. 161–171.

84. R. N. Filer and J. Ewalt. "State Hospitals as Domiciliary Care Facilities. In STATE MENTAL HOSPITALS, J. A. Talbott, ed. (New York: Human Sciences Press, 1980). Chapter 11, pp. 172–180.

85. F. N. Arnoff. Social Consequences of Policy Toward Mental Illness, *Science* 188 (1975) 1277–1281.

86. M. J. Eaton, M. H. Peterson and J. A. Davis. *Psychiatry: Medical Outline Series.* (New York: Medical Examination Publishing Company, 1981). pp. 487–489.

ACKNOWLEDGMENTS TO CONTRIBUTORS

The program of the Group for the Advancement of Psychiatry, a nonprofit, tax exempt organization, is made possible largely through the voluntary contributions and efforts of its members. For their financial assistance during the past fiscal year in helping it to fulfill its aims, GAP is grateful to the following:

Abbott Laboratories
American Charitable Foundation
Dr. and Mrs. Jeffrey Aron
Dr. and Mrs. Richard Aron
Virginia & Nathan Bederman Foundation
Ciba Pharmaceutical Company
Maurice Falk Medical Fund
Geigy Pharmaceuticals
Mrs. Carol Gold
The Gralnick Foundation
The Grove Foundation
The Holzheimer Fund
The Island Foundation
Ittleson Foundation, Inc., for Blanche F. Ittleson Consultation Program
Marion E. Kenworthy-Sarah H. Swift Foundation, Inc.
Lederle Laboratories
NcNeil Laboratories
Merck, Sharp & Dohme Laboratories
Merrell-National Laboratories
Phillips Foundation
Sandoz Pharmaceuticals
The Murray L. Silberstein Fund (Mrs. Allan H. Kalmus)
The Smith Kline Corp.
Mr. and Mrs. Herman Spertus
E.R. Squibb & Sons, Inc.
Jerome Stone Family Foundation
Tappanz Foundation
van Ameringen Foundation
Mr. S. Winn
Wyeth Laboratories